PENELOPE SHUTTLE

A LEAF OUT OF HIS BOOK

OxfordPoets
CARCANET

First published in 1999 by
Carcanet Press Limited
4th Floor, Conavon Court
12–16 Blackfriars Street
Manchester M3 5BQ

A CIP catalogue record for this book
is available from the British Library
ISBN 1 903039 00 2

The publisher acknowledges financial assistance
from the Arts Council of England

Set in 10pt Bembo by Bryan Williamson, Frome
Printed and bound in England by SRP Ltd, Exeter

For Peter and Zoe

and in memory of my cousin James Gunnell

Contents

Acknowledgements

Grateful acknowledgements are made to the following magazines and anthologies in which some of the poems have already appeared: *Acumen, The Affectionate Punch, Ambit, The Independent, The Interpreter's House, Links, London Magazine, The Manhattan Review, New Writing 6, Orbis, Poetry London Newsletter, Poetry Review, The Rialto, The Review, Rustic Rub, Southfields, Stand, Terrible Work, Times Literary Supplement, Verse* and *Writing Women.*

'Riddle' was commissioned for the *New Exeter Book of Riddles.*
'Scholar's Shop' and 'After Red' were commissioned for *Last Words* (Salisbury Poetry Festival).

The author gratefully acknowledges the financial assistance of The Authors' Foundation.

Adela *

I'm calmed by the image
of voyage,

who is not?
By distances of water

travelled
in a chapel of sail,

the canvas twanging and cracking
with oracular grumbles

in the mid-atlantic's
moody shove and repulse;

along the coast
all day is spent waiting,

until a shadow is found
at length

to be a ship,
that horizon glimpse

the nick of her hull,
those shimmer-stems her masts –

in a concourse of muscling sail
she knuckles over the gold sea plain's

finishing line of The Lizard,
sails in which not only the wind

---

* *The Adela*:   winner of the Atlantic Challenge Cup 1997,
raced from New York to The Lizard/Falmouth, Cornwall.

but light and shadow
are thrown and caught,

punted about,
protean and pulsing,

Bella Adela,
undulant winner,

Aphrodite ship
flying above the wave,

homing home
on an Aphrodite breeze.

The Anemometer

All summer,
each stroke of its luck recorded,

every breath noted,
each and every wind flying over the fig trees

and the jasmine,
those puffs of pearly gale

that loiter for days off-shore,
then rush inland, over foundered roses;

all its arabesque paths,
willing or unwilling,

committed to paper
by the anemometer on the roof

of a many-sided house on Western Terrace;
the wind pegged out and published on a graph,

no more secrecy,
the unseen is driven into sight,

detected trail of an ever-mobile mind,
direction and force and habits of the wind:

but best go back into the field
where the flowers are, these anemones,

bright slipshod daughters of the wind.

Penelope

All is made by the design of my hand.
What I weave is where and how he travels.
He sails on glittering tides I weave.
This skein is his hero's skin.

It is I who weave the web of spears.

Legend diminished me to wife
of the house, subject to suitors
and son: but my husband's life
hung from the thread coaxing through my fingers.

I spun his yarns, wove him by day,
unwove him by night, safe from harm.
I told them it was his father's shroud.
Women still see themselves in mirrors of my name.

I bend over my loom
and throw my shuttle, weaving
the world, its weathers,
its wise and unwise ways,

weaving your names, casting my
namesakes back into the web that flows
so fast from my ravelling hands.
Over my face they pinned a veil of lies.

But it was made by the design of my hand.

Infanta

The first time I hold her
is two days
after an emergency caesarean,
delivery that felt more
like a road accident
than a birth,
she studies me silently,
memorizing my face,
her gaze unastonished, replete,
eyes grey in a wax-yellow face —
(all the other babies
are scarlet as if furious
or embarrassed or both,
but a nurse tells me
all caesareans are pale).
On this winter morning,
the hospital lawn
white with frost's lunar suddenness,
the future shines so brightly
and fearfully around us both
I can't see into it —
twenty years later
this day is out of reach
of my grown daughter's memory
but to me it is still the latest news,
her infant weight
still a hot heavy surprise in my arms,
and despite the unstoppable surge
of time,
here I am, always,
with her,
at the same door of hurt and hope,
two people in a miracle room
where those who can
cast away their crutches,
plaster casts, white sticks,
and we do.

Pistil Meadow, The Lizard

A little fearful river
hurrying back to sea,
a new stair in the green cliff –
between them

the quiet tamarisk grove,
willowy stems, long feathery
pink racemes . . .
Pistil or Pistol Meadow

where in 1720 they buried
so many drowned soldiers
out of the 'Royal Anne';
only two out of two hundred

survived the wreck,
the rest washed up at low tide,
weed-wreathed, clodged
with sand, wedged in culverts

and shafts of razoring rock,
and with them
a cargo of pistols,
severe spoils:

days it took
to carry the poor naked bodies
up to the barren meadow
and bury them –

dogs from up to twenty miles away
came to feast on the unburied –
years later
you could walk all across the Lizard

and never hear one farmyard bark,
such appetite unforgiven;
today
in foraging mists and scrimped hazes,

walking down the stepped cliff
and over the grassy hussocks
of the long-weathered burial pit,
you would not know it was here,

so many bones under the sighing tamarisk,
beside the growling sea.

Vanity

My poor old breasts,
soft and flat and sunken

as two ineptly-cooked
yorkshire puddings,

empty old breasts
well-read but floppy,

as lax and loose
as gone-elastic

left in a sad drawer,
sulky pair,

six months older
than the breasts

of the mistress
of the Prince of Wales,

shifty customers:
but you kiss them,

you say – no, not so,
as peachy and girl-firm

as ever . . .
You liar,

kissing old breasts
that can still blush

into mothiness.

Eclipse

Weatherwise, we are more anxious
than for an only child's wedding,
or an outdoor fête

at which a royal threatens to appear,
this fête of fêtes,
the eclipse, total and in preparation

for seventy years.
We need clear skies, we need
the weather to sit tight and be good.

'How can I express the darkness?
It was a sudden plunge
when one did not expect it;

being at the mercy of the sky . . .'
Virginia Woolf,
eclipse-watching in 1927.

As our eclipse ripens
the first landfall of darkening
will be Land's End,

one by one the b and b villages
of the Peninsula –
Madron, Zennor and Goldsithney,

Manaccan, St Keverne, Breage
and Pampaluna – will go dark. Just after
breakfast Godolphin Hill will vanish,

and then Falmouth,
so often by so many
sailed around, now to be sailed

into a rare dark
at the noon height of the beach-partying day,
by a night out of sequence,

wandering the worlds,
resistless. This is the event
that must be looked at aslant or askance,

through special goggles,
like amateur welders,
or by any curious avoidance device,

just as Dad in 1944
in his jungle prison camp at Chungkai
saw an eclipse of the sun

reflected in the water
from the River Kwai
with which speculum he'd filled his army haversack.

Valentine for a Dinosaur

Because you still take up more than your fair share,
old bone-marshall,
beloved time-sobered creature;

because you once tore through thwacked valleys
or sat your turn, faithful partner, on a château-nest
under the flying colours of your rainbow plumes,

uttering the fortissimo of your unrecorded songs;
because of the untiring way you entertain me
with your bigness, your boney communion;

because of the glint of an invisible eye
in your scoured eyesocket
aloft in its museum lookout, and because

you still possess all the caprice
of a true thoroughbred, I love you
and your survivor's expeditious stance,

your calcite repose,
the circus-gloss of each black-varnished bone,
reliable and abiding articulation,

but most of all, Dinosaur, I love
the warm strokeable dimpled boulder
of your aloe-coloured longevity shit,

this solid jet bowling ball of coprolite,
to me, the luckiest love charm, a lover's ultimate amulet.

Trophy

Doffed in death,
a coat of many browns,

'zigzags of effulgence',
amber and tobacco body suit

of the shrew mouse,
one of the busy kindred

of the long snouts,
belly of erminish-tint,

soft as eider,
back fur a smoothwork of mossy jet,

tail a minute whip
or disciplinarian for elves,

a clean cat kill
on the massacre lawn,

not a mark on
the ever-assenting victim,

shrew paws curled in consent,
or as if entrusted mouseishly

with many never-given-away secrets,
tiniest of trophies,

briefest entry in a game book,
burial a minute's work,

a scraped hole
by the scarlet indifferent roses

blooming bigger and better
each year

from elixir of shrew
at their roots.

Shoes of the Rose

A rose,
enjoying its own shadow,

its privacy of thorns,
its livelihood of scents,

gravities and zests
of the rain.

Overlooked usher
of the forest,

choosing the luck
of the forgotten,

reaping the rewards
of reclusion;

anyone might like
to step into the shoes

of the rose.

Scholar's Shop

He has farewells
like jewels,
he has thoughts like a tree
of thoughts,
or like little crusts of bread,
he has books of a calmness
not to be found anywhere else. Yet
he is as a false jewel
to himself, a sky unfolded without thought.
He has continuance,
like the sun or the moon.
He has Venice and Genoa
for shield and protection. He has hope
in the form of a globe. He has storms,
like riches. He assembles in crowds,
in leapyear biographies. He washes over me
in faiths of water, frosts of light,
cloud-memoirs. He shows me
how to design a peach, how to find
a landscape not yet two years old,
he is progressive as a comet,
sparkling, icy, all tail and purpose,
or wears his bird mask
to build an aviary by the sea.
He has farewells like patience,
like all the world's colours appearing before their judge.

Tolgus

An inch of tin concentrate
in a tiny glass tube
stoppered with cork
like a wine of rareness —

very very dry.

I mine this tin
from her lode of unwanted toys,
a box of bow-legged wind-up mice,
barbie bras and non-jumping frogs.

For years it has been in the dark,
grey grit
smaller than sandgrains,
with a shimmer more like moondust

than clean particles of tin
first ferreted out at Tolgus,
ground-up and roasted
like a mineral coffee,

a beverage
that could only be drunk by a god —
Jupiter, say —
tin always loved him.

Tolgus is a Cornish tin mine.

Herbal Warfare

A wartime appeal:
send us
one thousand tons of dried nettles.

Anyone who has,
anyone who is willing to learn
herb recognition.

At once
an army of gloved gatherers
the length and breadth

of the cut-off country –
schoolchildren,
devotees, recluses,

the rank-and-file left-at-homes –
got busy harvesting
the neglect of hedges,

wastelands,
ditches which nettles love best
and where they grow best.

*

The nettle's juice
is bottle green,
melancholy's green:

from its weasel-scented seepings
comes a gift,
the dye of camouflage,

nature's counterfeit.
An 'ever-growing band
of plant enthusiasts'

sent in ninety tons
of this
'flimsy-leaved uncomfortable plant',

the Stinging, the Roman,
and the Little Annual Nettle,
eight pounds of fresh leaves

yielding less
than one pound
of the dried herb.

Remember the princess
who wove nettle shirts
for the eleven swans, her brothers?

Soon tanks snuck
in under camouflage cloaks,
soldiers wore leafgreen

invisibility uniforms,
nettle tea and nettle beer
gave their strengthening iron

to the warrior drinkers;
and in 1941
under the 'vigilant

and untiring' organization
of Dr Butcher
the herboristes collected

over ten tons
of miscellaneous herbs –
a 'noble and most exhausting task';

but a record year
for the young British herb industry.
In 1942

one thousand tons
of Horse Chestnuts,
and as many of Rose Hips . . .

By now each region specialized:
Wales and the West Country
had the bounty

of foxgloves,
towering, quaintly-rosetted,
its tiny multitudinous seeds

seeking the heart:
Sussex and Rutland replenished
supplies of Belladonna,

Male Fern
hurried from Northumberland,
other shires sent Henbane,

that ugly smelly soother
of labour pains,
easer also of seasickness

for the invasion troops;
and everywhere-Yarrow, with its thousand leaves;
(backalong, Achilles

healed his soldiers with this vulnerary,
Herba militaris;)
prickly Thornapple arrived,

a narcotic, an alleviator,
like Belladonna;
efficacious Vervain

to cool fevers,
(with bunches of which
the Romans swept their altars);

and seaweed
from the coastal districts,
thirty-three tons in 1944 alone,

to help with the magical succade –
called Penicillin –
born from an alliance

of waves, storms, rocks;
saving lives and comforting many:
from two seaweeds – Gigartina and Chondrus,

garnered amid biting storms,
in salt-choked air,
slippery in stinging hands,

evasive,
a wrack of healing there –
for without this Agar Agar

herborized from the seaweed
'experimental work
would have been seriously hampered . . .'

So into the Ministry of Health
came the pharmacopoeia of the wild,
the amateur army

somehow overcoming
the pre-central-heating era difficulties
of finding good drying places,

dispatching the herbs upcountry
in good wellwoven burlaps,
the sacks safely tied,

or sent in tins and boxes
lined with brown paper;
comfrey's crushed leaves, mildly scented,

the paper-thin leaves of lime,
the bee-beloved lime,
nerve-soother;

a ransom of herbs
paid in time of war,
supplying 'the nation's medicine chest'.

Source of information and quotations: Florence Ranson, *British Herbs* (Pelican Books, 1949).

Nail

Soberness of a small nail,
a nymph of steel,
of usefulness,

of grace, of favour –
crumb from a bread
of stiff charity,

minute spike of mercy,
but,
unlike a needle,

blind,
waiting for any hammer,
any wall,

longing to travel,
monogamous,
into the ardour of dark.

At Kynance Cove, Lizard Peninsula, Cornwall

High above the rocks at Kynance,
one star, o little powerful one,
midsummer silver. O dust of small vexations,
jumps of judgement.
Only ever one phoenix, one joy.
And after Kynance
a room with a domed ceiling
on which stars and planets
gradually appeared, bright and special.
A plan of how to live.
There was no fear in the spirit.
There was a love of different times
of day, there was always a sea
calm and flat and blue as a wound-drink.
Hills and clouds
of tenderest gravity.
There was a present of poems
and seaweed from my poet.
'The beautiful tombs of Eleusis,
the marble sheaves and the lotus'.
Our selves revisited,
again and again. In forgotten houses
the pirouette of weather
mindreading through the walls.
Curious weather,
its many minds,
pencilling-in a sigh here,
a shiver there.
Sometimes bringing a bad thought.
Perhaps it is a thought everyone has.
Perhaps it is only my thought.
Swiftly I exchange my thought for
some beautiful English pondweed: Small Frog's Lettuce.
I exchange my thought for this star,
such consenting light,
such fruits everywhere, given away free.

Gaston Bachelard notes that in the time of Descartes a pirouette meant a weathervane.

Verdant

Leaf masks on the portal

A mask of leaves,
secret faces,
faces under the leaves,
or of the leaves,
puzzle faces,
fountains of leaves springing,
spraying from wide mouths
whose speech is a green and silent spray,
echo of unsungness

The forest where every leaf has its own smell,
its green repertorium,
has come indoors
into the tall broad stone houses,
the barns of holiness or habit
and the faces scowl from their leaf beards,
their tendril moustaches,
the men of green, the silvanae
in from the boudoirs of thunder and forest rain,
and what they don't know about good and evil
isn't worth knowing

*

Faces of abasement?
Or
garlanded?

*

Grief
in the leaf face,
as if
saying farewell
to human form —

and feeling as they do
more human than ever,
surging back
from stone
to forest shape
and back to stone again –
to watch us
from portal,
capital,
frieze, pillar,
as if to see if we can become leaf

*

'beautiful deformities;
                    deformed beauties'
Arbor mala
        and *Arbor bona*
Tête de Feuilles
            Masque Feuillu
                    Masque Herbu

*

Human faces turning to leaves
Leaf faces becoming human
My face prickling with leaves,
acanthus, vines –
will my tongue flower?

*

leaf demons
leaf angels

leaves as if blown
into disorder
by a forsaking wind

*

Hawthorn masks
blossoming,
and tiny dragons
with tails of white may

*

Foliage faces of salutation,
hieratic, compassionate,
anticipatory —
as if about to blurt out secrets
by word of leaf mouth —

leaf-rustle-speech
A parley of green discourse

Or as if what they knew
was too much for us to bear

so they stay silent
they bear it for us
half hidden in stone
subversive among hymns
leaf-reticent
still buddhas of grief

*

Here
where nature rises up
as if to speak
yet waits and waits,
speech turned to stone

As eyes open
in the stone

and stone tongues
stretch out silence

Many faces
in the leaves

Some faces smiling,
but never the eyes

Bramble sprays bursting
from ears,
from mouths . . .

A gout of leaves
from a mouth,
a prophecy? a promise?
leaf-logos?

*

On my way home from school
I gathered leaves, my favourites,
acacia, elm,
laid them down
at the foot of special trees,
it was comforting,
it felt right,
for I was taking a leaf
out of the green man's book

*

Face to face
with the green man,
his green mirror

*

At Winterbourne Monkton
the woman on the font
is giving birth to leaves,
she has been

37

mutilated
so we shall not know
she is a goddess
but
there she is,
as are the mermaids
in a church in France
whose split scaly fishtails
burst into oceanic leaf

*

Leafmasks once painted bright
as Hindu shrines

But goldleaf sometimes —
exuberant, paradisal —
still circles the faces
that are then one face

*

Our green mirrors,
reflections,
our kindred spirits,
our husbands,
our brothers,
these vernal men,
stone icons,
asleep in the stone
with eyes wide open,
green shadows, green
consorts, viriditas

*

In churches, cathedrals and abbeys
the leaf lord —

like that essential flaw in the perfect pattern
where life breaks through

*

A poet* dressed in ivy
addressing his words of greeting
to the Queen at Kenilworth
in 1575; in her dress of *Amor en fleur*,
all verdant and upright
in leafy brocades of royal leisure

*

le fou conceals himself
in the fragrant field of uncut grass,
hiding and seeking

le fou,
the fool green as grass,
the no-fool he

You'll see him also
in a church by the sea,
carved in wood

dark as dusk in a forest,
eyes closed,
head hooded in a cock's comb,

fool crowned with beak,
wattle,
and pinpoint averse eye

Foolscap

---

* George Gascoigne (1534–77)

Also he holds a wand
carved with his own face
again bird-hooded

When the scythe-men come
to harvest the hay,
the fool in his folly still plays

All the life flies out of the field,
mice, hares, toads, spiders,
even snails must hurry –

But le fou hides,
the curved blades seek,
cut him down to size,

fool who loves to live
but not forever
in his fool's paradise,

his blood rushing off on its fool's errand,
his cheerful bones eked out;
such is the charity of the fool,

such
is the fool's
'quality of unexpectedness . . .'

*

'the leaves that issue
from the Green Man's mouth
are an answering song
or incantation
in which the spirits of trees
speak to man'

*

And in London we looked up
and saw the friezes and cornices
where the leafy faces quickened
high above the fumes and despairs

*

Summer Lord, May King,
yet consort of a greater

*

The green face of Osiris
after his resurrection
and his chosen life
in the underworld,
'A green thought
in a green shade'

his fingers fold fast into leaves
stalks spring from his eyes

choosing freely
to be lord of a green underworld
among the hiding and seeking souls

Background information and quotations are from: William Anderson, *Green Man* (Harper Collins, 1990) and Kathleen Basford, *The Green Man* (D.S. Brewer Ltd, 1978).

Mother and Daughter
for Z

In those days
I was entrusted with a waterfall
purer than St Nectan

or any other
that had a woman's name,
then, as now,

between afternoon
and evening, I studied
the songs

of the young waterfall
as closely
as my own cascade-acoustics allowed,

or
as the brush-footed butterflies did,
in airy precipitant good-tempers;

for in those days
I was also an Undine,
like my waterfall child:

you could see
the wet of our footprints
race across the clouds

and how
in the throes of our rainbows
we digressed into twilight

just for the fun of it,
untroubled
by talk of the end of the world . . .

for a wealth of water
sheltered
this young investor of ours:

then one waterfall
went travelling far and wide,
her fountains

around her
like so many fluid suitors,
while I waited out

the puzzle of my drought
until today
when

in the rippling bowl
of her hands
she brings me lasting water.

My Son

My son is one of those stars
painted on the silk star chart
made in Dunhuang in 940 AD,

he is one of the doves hidden
but vocal in the ragged three-storeyed
dove-cote along the lane,

he is also a racing pigeon
circling with many others
when my furthest neighbour

casts and twirls his lasso of birds
heavenward,
tugging the sky into a treble noose of noise,

unison that puzzled me so much
buzzing over the garden
like an invisible top, till I understood

his pigeons wore ankle whistles
to make the sky sing,
and when he calls them down –

'come back, come back', into the loft
they obey
in reluctant sky-loving batches,

the last one in is my son;

sometimes though
he is an eskimo curlew,
Numenius borealis, almost extinct,

flying over the Hold-with-Hope
Peninsula –
in his bird's eye view

has all the luminous tradition
of the Arctic,
leaping ice, water and light,

mirages, refractions,
wing shadow on ice,
silk star on silk sky,

for he is of that upper element,
he is far yet near,
never yet forever

descending from his flight,
his weight barely grazing me,
alighting in my arms

then relaunching,
will not be called back
from his wherever

among all the other unborn,
winging from me again,
his name as in silk spun from my tongue.

Gifts and Forfeits

The mirror;
as spiritual apology.

The liar's
costly long-run.

The customary loneliness
of a swan.

Childhood
that does not end at night.

The banished vermilion
of a rose.

A spider
walking on plums.

The rain's child
stealing a mountain.

A spare set of nipples,
the design

simple yet effective.
A hospital clown,

distracting the sick.

Frogs

My frogs
maketh a noise-music for me

in the mists of an ordinary
garden. My answering dance

is a locomotion of great beauty,
sporadically applauded

by frogs. Fresh croaking begins:

Ego alas, ego alas.

Eighteen Rains

1
The old handle-less blue jug
left out all night,

its netted glaze
dim in bunching drifting shadows;

old, cracked and sage,
it fills up with rain,

little aged sanctuary.
At dawn I water our newborn strawberries,

pouring out the rains of providence.

2
Rain without thunder,
a strong rain fit to impregnate the oysters
in their Helford beds.
Nature's healthy sorcery
loudly at work wakes me,
the dawning room pries me
from shell of dream . . .

3
Rain-licker river,
lingerer among shimmer
and plume of rain.
Sleepwalker through big clouds
asleep with rain.

4

Swaying delphinia,
dank blue garden gossamers,
leaf-masks, thin unrests of light,
vert, le jade,
a little weeping horse:
he also is the rain.

5

Rain,
following the bull
because he is thinking about flowers:

hum of rain where north and south meet.

6

Eligible ponds and secluded cataracts
of an early un-named lover of rain,

one who asks only
for the repose of rain.

7

A red rose in a dark vase
on a twilit table.
The rain, unheard of.

8

Tall rain rising from the lakes
in hushes of amber;

sunstruck waters like sleeping silks
fallen from favour.

49

9

One raindrop –
a pearl bred in the smallest river
in the world
in whose gleam a messenger
is stranded.

10

The rain carries her eyes home
in a dish
through the dew and sweat of dawn,

a crown of lost chances
shining on her poor head.

11

Some days,
more rain than we know what to do with;
enough rain to fill the dark hangar
of a cathedral, douse its multiple candles
(lit for the dead, who haul from us
still our homage, our obeisance):

12

enough rain to wash clean
a cathedral of muddy altars.
Let it be done by candlelight,
let the dead help.

13

One fountain,
the living saint of the rain.

14

A chalk and lily cloud;
rustling oblivions of rain,

15

through which the honey
of a cool summer may be tasted.

16

A masterpiece discovered
in cobweb corner
long after the painter is dead:

rain falling at such a moment
is called: Dutch rain.

17

O who lets such sweet weather
continue?

18

Rain's beautiful brogue,
its culminant song.
Its dazzle-texts and good tidings;

it gives lessons in mirage
to the watermeadows:
that is why their green is griefless.

My Parents

My parents
touring woods and fields
in sunlight,

touring for pleasure,

willing to show
the world
to any.

Where they go,
trees and flowers
boast of knowing them,

my parents,

even the big bright
bashful summer clouds.

Z's Gift to P

Echinocorys scutata,
sea urchin nuzzled into stone,

burrower into time,
traveller past time,

worn smooth in one of the world's
uttermost pockets or pouches,

so long under the sea,
under soft hoof of octopus,

long flapping rug of giant ray,
fathomless but never out of your depths,

once regarded as a fairy loaf,
stone that if kept in the larder

promised unfailing bread,
this long-distance gift

from daughter to father
had its millionth birthday

ten million years ago,
wishes you, Dad, many happy returns.

Because 'n'

Because n has fallen on his side
and become z,
because g has forgotten what sex he or she is,
and because l
has run out of voices
and q has gone to live overseas,
tired of being p's mirror,
because a is now available only
in standard sizes,
and b is liable to freeze up;
because m and h
are losing weight and not sleeping,
because d thinks he owns all the rivers,
while y is making fans
in the comfort of her own home;
because f is picking up the smallest sounds
on her shadow
and o is increasingly remote;
because r is hanging upside down
in a vain attempt to save space
and s is still sleeping on his back;
because c is memory-challenged,
and because t is down-loading and home-shopping,
because i is ideal when travelling alone,
because u is clean-tempered as the air
when it sees ice crystals clinging
to the sides of a fence,
because v is open to persuasion,
because x is happiest folded flat,
because e and j are thinking over the events
of the last fifty years,
and k is always hiding behind the door,
you can guess from all this
that Dufy is writing a letter to his daughters,
each a or b or c, or x or y or z
a versus or a revision
tumulting down the page

in a calligraphy of colours
lit up by the same courteous articulate light
that rains its cursive rainbows
and fortune-de-mer blues
down forever over the towers of the Château du Saumur.

A Sleeve's Mood

A sleeve's mood, like a leaf
or lip guarding the memoir,
or a pendulum
that takes a nap, or smiles,
as it tours its veils,
its forgery books, its handles
that froth up, or re-organizes
all the whys and wherefores
of its newly-discovered mathematics,
and adds to the premise
of each interlude
as it dissolves something
that is falling like rain
but is not rain, for it omits
all its hyphens, like an unbearable
orchard,
and is not a pretty little room
on a winter night
where on a large square table
a glass of water
gets lonelier and lonelier
studying an ancient language.

A Future for Cornwall

Let Penzance wither on its hook.
Let the dust lick and nibble Bodmin.
Let all the windows close on Truro.
Let Falmouth stoop over.

Let cloud work out what to do with Kynance.
Let the rain select its own towns.
Let the untaught waterfalls solve
the traffic problems of Wadebridge.

Let the horses of Par forget their ambitions,
but let the dogs of Veryan
dance as they have always done.
Let the babies of Gweek forget their former lives.

Let tears be brought, at last, to Godolphin.
Let spiders overtake Redruth.
Let the sky lift her dark hands over Goldsithney.
Let St Ives be blessed with a sullen and gallant pearl.

Let the ant rule Madron,
and let the barbaric geishas of Roseland,
aloof in their blooms of saffron and bronze,
learn to like a quiet life.

Les Reines

The rains of circumstance.
Or the rain
that falls from a cloudless sky,
neither frivolous nor ceremonious.
A soul made of hands,
the sanity produced by weeping.
My most private thoughts.
Secrecy of water under bridges.
Light, rain and mist.
Heat-haze and silence.
A sunlit tempest.
Jade and ice, spit and frost.
Leaves of the silver birches
smoking with light.
Echo and contradiction.
Such backwards flowering,
and late signs.
Sour-leafed sorrel,
sinewy sisal.
Spurts of tenderness
for such harsh plants,
for junk gardens.
Wind rocks the fig tree,
the great openhand leaves
show their furry undersides,
their glossy upper surfaces
piqued and rummaged.
Winds whip the waters,
to bring rain.
There is also the singing part
of the world.
And the clean water
of the little river
at Restronguet
as it ran out —
sibilance from under the hill,
red leaves aswirl,

and at St Genny's
in nightwind and cold
how the stars shot up –
jets of whiteness
against black brilliance!
O dew frost,
O blossom tree,
O things done without pretext,
as the world weakened by us
moves on,
webs of small spiders
floating in calms of autumn,
and queens without feet
in scarlet petticoats,
arms lifted all day, all night,
('seeds by the thousand
fly with the wind'),
les reines, sweet rosebay,
welcome us and let us go.

'seeds by the thousand . . .': Geoffrey Grigson, *The Englishman's Flora* (Phoenix House, 1958).

Bulletin d'Expédition

1
Buddha's big frown:
this planet of trash and thorns!
No greenworld . . .

2
Seven stepping stones
in a frozen stream;
snow on the white-painted beehives of St Cleer.

3
Soft thunk-thunk
of ripe figs
falling on your paved yard.

4
River,
patient eavesdropper;
daylight of Wednesday, fading.

5
Hand in hand
he steps with the angel
caught by the charm
of the unearthly one.

6
My ghostly bi-sexual dog.
I call him
Tobias; my black pet.

7
A hundred dancing pharaohs.
Solomon's
bird language.
Singing trees alope with light.

8
Fear;
glinting sweetness
within the nutshell.

9
Loudest sound?
Sea breeze
through the thistles.

10
The seas re-sexed,
but love
still only going one way.

11
Dog-wedding
on a street corner;
no invitations, no
speeches.

12
A sky
with its own attitude
to dance and sexuality.

13
Shadow footsteps
in the unhappy kitchen;
her endless convalescence.

14
A gardener's fate;
silver-leaf tree aquiver
by stone well.

15
Fast-lane nightmare,
producing a fiery image of the Pope.

16
The green pearl of clairvoyance.
The rabble of amorous children.

17
The ghosts of Coronation St
glide away
over the waste tips.

18
Reine Solus,
wet and reckless with dew.

19
Smell of afternoon spiders;
a scarlet and gold childhood,
the little king's accomplice.

20
She smiles but not at me
in our echo palace.

21
Big glassy sleep-pigs,
big depleting sleep-swine,
pig-pearls of slumber . . .

22
Rain on the attic roof;
I raise my hand
to ward off a volley of pearls.

23
I dream all in black
and every morning
I bleach those dreams white
for many reasons.

24
Casino-glitter
of the sunset rainshow:
my shirt blister-dabbed
with big wet drops.

25
Ladder,
the eloper's essential prop,
magical runged ascensional path.

26
Or, ladder as sketch
of or draft for true stairs,

outdoor cousin
of inner steps.

27
Light's glitter patchwork
stretched over seven mirrors
in one of which
lulled lilies also rise
white and too big to hide.

28
In a hundred cradles
babies with milk-blister lips
are already turning into men.

29
Strange unpredictable acoustics
of snow,
like people singing chinese
Beethoven,
Ode to Joy
at a Qingdao wedding.

30
Wet roofs climb west.
Like distant events in other lives.

31

Washing up the stolen lunchboxes
in her sweet-tooth kitchen,
Midasina, her golden lips,
her golden gloves.

32

In the Year of the Octopus
I follow all the weathers of China,

all my arms reaching out for hugs
to the faraway child

sleeping in the Orient as I wake,
who wakes when I sleep in the Occident.

33

We must make room for him
on the sofa,
even though he is someone else's wizard.

34

Oh my tall blue-eyed Goethes,
your heartbeats,
your comradely pats and nudges
as we walk together fast over city bridges!

35

Some armchairs are so comfy
they are not able
to live ordinary lives.

36
Flower snail
in the cool evening,
plus six white rose-ghosts
lost in thought and rain.

37
'Little-known riches
in royal hands . . .'

38
(And waking from the dreamtime
the two selves
change places in the driving seat . . .)

39
Somebody who sometimes
comes to visit
with her pop-up book
of air disasters and motorway pile-ups,
always arrives calling out –
'Blessings on this house!'

40
Out of the train window:
cities and moorland
and night smelling of sparks,
of struck flint,
every now and then,
green sparks, sudden flares
and flashes of fire
in the dark.

41

A town with too many bookshops,
where darkness arrives
as an adult, sex unknown,

42

where the books fly by,
and foxes fly by reading them,
the children like this.

43

. . . the streets of St Blazey
white with unforecast snow,
the work of a devotee,

44

my sleepy benefactor,
who tells me:
The roof has to be mended.
It has to be mended truthfully.
Only my lover can do it.

Ultra Sound

But I only looked at the screen
when the doctor asked the nurse –
freeze that, will you?

And saw a smoky sea roaring
silently inside my breast,
a kneading ocean of echo-scape,

resonant-surge of sombre waves,

like the Falmouth sea
at autumn twilight, smudge
of grey surfs and bruise-black billows,

grainy shadow-sea inside me,
soundless thump
of seismic wave after wave

breaking over two black rocks,
harmless cysts,

and below, mute, storm-bleak,
the long black trembling scarp of suspect tissue.

Hope

Either there are no bridges,
or too many bridges.

Either no river,
or too many rivers.

Either there's a pack of Macbeths,
better at entrances than exits,

or one indescribable hero
shielding his face from the sun.

Either he speaks the truth,
or a burlesque of sweet yellow lies.

Either the world swings round
moored on its own name,

or it has no name;
either it is fading to that green

of the long pointed leaves you feed to silkworms,
or blue

as a shadow healing the sick,
or,

like a painter of roses,
it burns, anonymous in reds and thorns.

Things

The little lost book.
A lorry full of chairs, so silent,

a plague inspector's mood.
One of the masks of requirement,

a little path through the trees,
but oh so beautiful,

the example, shining.

Any man may close his eyes,
but still the flower opens,

its thistly leaf brims
with tickle hairs,

its small milk-yellow petals
arch in perpetual downiness,

it is another of the things
heaven paints in secret,

and loses.

Silence Could Not Believe

I took silence out of doors
to show it things
before they wane,
undescribing and taking
the plurals for granted,
adding shivers to them
sometimes –
but
silence could not believe
the sea just went on
being the sea
nor that the land
would step back like that
to watch it happening,
also
silence had no idea
there would be a taste
in the air
of ripe plums
growing on trees
along a pilgrim path
from stones spat out
hundreds of years ago,
nor
that the dusk
would suddenly open
like a book
in a silence all its own.

Sight Seeing

A waterlily
torchlit for decades

or the mane and eyes
of the eighth

most valuable child
in the world

or a woodcut
of country air,

portraits
of free and easy archaeologists,

one hundred mice
en route from China

to Paris
in a night rush

of agued whiskers,

seeking out young wives of thunder,
the apricot silk

of their best bed gloves
made just for sleeping in.

Bayleaf

Wild garlic,
blue harebells,

fleurs du bois,
fleurs du champ,

one sharp-scented –
a non-culinary herb

but smelling medicinal
enough to chill out

a hangover,
the bluebells

scentless as individuals
but

as a community
achieving a perfume

that aspires up
to re-tune and pleasure

the air so frankly
it is reason alone

for the creation
of noses here

along the green path
beyond the dockyard

where
the worn-out battleship

Bayleaf,
blotched, sea-lichened

like an old fighting shark,
is dry-docked for a refit,

six months work
for 300 men in mostly unwaged times,

from whose hull
eddies of astringent oil

and caustic paint,
reek of burnt lime

and seep of sulphates
sun-shiver

into clear blue salt air
and out

over the estuary
and its long spring-green hills:

acidic stars oddly seen
in a daytime

spray-burst
out of the welder's thumbs,

his stellar work
in bursts of white gold,

fire sparks
steadily flowering

their burn-your-eye-out petals,
their look-away-quick blooms.

Two Visits to the Men-an-Tol, West Penwith, Cornwall

Ishmael's Shaft, Hard Shaft and Robin's Shaft,
long disused now, mere falls of shadow and air
into tunnelled earth, wickered-over with keep-out lids,

but the abandoned engine houses around Bodrifty
and Little Galver glitter charmed lives in holiday sun
under a clear wildblue sky as we approach

the stones moored in the moorland;
years ago, on our first visit, mist looms
wove and unwove luminous chilly muslins of fog

over the gorseland
out of which the three stones suddenly blossomed,
two waist-high pillars, to east and west,

and between them,
forever motionlessly circling,
a holed stone big enough for anyone to look out or in,

holy stone and her two sentinel sisters.
(Who said at night they run to the river and drink,
or dance across the brazen moor,

hopping over the laid-stone hedges?)
Twenty years ago I clambered through the maw
of the mother stone, entering, travelling, exiting

three times,
the rabbit-mown grass scratchy on my knees
as I crawled through, against the clouded sun,

through this granite polo-mint mother,
or giantess-bracelet of stone,
cervix-anchor steadying me in a sea of mist and gorse,

the mass of her cold and rough to my touch,
like a fallen moon, stone ball of string,
ravelling and unravelling in stillness –

winding thousands of years of healing,
fertility and divination invisibly around herself
and her attendant pillars –

I threaded myself through the pierced stone,
my child within me not to be born for seven months yet;
fertile I was, blessing for the child I sought,

safe passage –
for first comes blossom, then bud, then fruit –
hoicked up into the world via meticulous hospital panics,

she arrived unharmed; and years later, at noon,
at the hot height of May, the coconut scent of the gorse
outfragrancing the salt of the sea,

drifting the yachts along in perfumed gales,
my daughter plunge-wriggles, coquets and corkscrews
herself through the granite o,

the ever-open place's massive orbit:
now it is she who will carry the cornucopia,
roped in her turn to earth and the spring.

Quicksilver House

This quicksilver house
keeps strictly to itself,
doesn't mix or mingle,

its liquidity
is one of the miracles
of nature, very great miracle,

at slightest nudge
the quicksilver house
runs in blobs and dabs and blendes,

tilting and recombining
with its one self in oneness,
a solid fluid,

doorways, windows and roof
spilling in mirror truancies
and weighty radiances,

a shining shelter,
a wetly-shattering and re-uniting home.

In All Weathers

A dream cannot procure you
wealth in the world

but it has a gilt-edged tongue,
is an arguer of luminous cunning,

shares out its riches
like any friend sharing sorrows
in all weathers.

God

Green sea and blue heaven.
Hot sun and cool tree.

The complete silence of Me
reflecting on my faults.

My faults?
I sit beside them, no more, no less.

They coil and doze and bask,
half-shadow, half-snake.

While the blue heaven
and the green sea

continue to provide Me
with the ideal weather of antiquity.

Scholarship

They arrive neck-first,
white-green napes pushing black earth aside.

Nasturtium, gourd-flower.

For a day and a night, the white necks shine,
while leafheads stay buried,

deep in earth, deep in thought,
tiny ostriches of the plant world.

Then each head rises, veined,
clean as a wiped knife.

Green stars of longevity bless
these yearly returners,

resuming their green scholarship again and again.

For Dimitri

I live in the former cosmonauts compound
but like most of the other residents

I hardly ever think
about those long-gone days of space travel.

Those superb rockets!
How they bankrupted us!

Sometimes at night I search the sky
for the fire-ribboned star of my son's space ship.

But only the splashdown moon
shrugs at me in Dimitri-mode,

still has no interest in politics . . .

Clever Ones

Many of the children of nineteenth-century concubines
in Brazil, Scotland and China

are naturally intelligent;
others are not.

The clever children like thunder,
his godship the fox, the shiver of a moon guitar.

But the stupid are happy also.

They like those long unworried clouds at sunset,
peach-red, the rose of tailors' chalk.

They like big rivers,
and temples where incense-doped vipers

wind around the legs of travelling clerics.

These the stupid admire,
while clever ones fly for their lives.

'Not an Exact Science . . .'

It is not an exact science.
No hints published in the Peking Gazette.

A whale swallowing a country,
green hills and blue towns,

that's something like it.
Or winning the rollover lottery, the big one.

A very narrow escape of one's life
is closer, perhaps.

Or learning to read,
ten years later than everyone else in school.

Or renaming a constellation:
'Pansie's Footsteps', say, or 'Beautiful Tongue'.

Because fucking is not an exact science.

Someone
for Z

Despite the tutelage of certain weathers,
a rainfall
terribly busy and satin polite,
the tiny art of snow,

someone thought of you, and such a thought –
like a childhood
you can use over and over again,
or that centuries-old Chinese admiration for pines.

Rainbow

In his bodice of light and rain
a rainbow
likes to be descended from the weatherside

of the world,
likes to be brief,
a student of the secretive,

a colour-merchant,
a road wide enough for the roomiest
of strolling lions,

so narrow
none but the proudest snake can pass.

In Hiding

Just as a dowser,
despite the hole in his fortune,

knows where the finest water lives,
and why it needs so much depth,

a ua de plus belle,
so I remember you

passing for rain
in your orchard,

amid your lakes in flight,
your lapinière of light,

your usable marvels:
beginning again and again,

but hidden as water hides,
in its modest science,

until found, or unfound,
as the world on its travels

wills.

Far in the East

In the very hot summers
of north-eastern China
(where you spent
most of this winter)

they used to keep ice
in big turquoise-lacquer chests
set in the middle of the rooms.
I saw one

in the Chinese Galleries
at the V and A,
close to some vivid embroidered robes
on which gold-sewn dragons

pursued pearls among clouds,
where five peaches
and five bats predicted
long life and happiness

on the unapproachable sleeves of robes
each big enough to wrap unruffled six Emperors –
(one looks back over his shoulder
at the moon in a niche of mist).

Nearby was a characteristic platform bed
straight out of a pillow book
(crammed with couches
where the man's Crimson Bird

flies swiftly into her Secret Cavern,
a pot of bamboo shoots
erectly by the window, paint brushes
and love cloths strewn about.)

Also I saw paintings of horses
and peonies –
and a thought
remembered from a book came to me –

that in China
painting is a devout non-figurative pursuit,
not so much concerned
with the reproduction of reality

as with the evocation of deep feeling
either
through meditation
or inebriation . . .

and all these sights, all these thoughts,
and so much more,
Zoe,

make your mother long for you,
travelling all these months
far from us in the East . . .

The Well at Mylor

At Mylor
the water of the well

bears the armour of the light,
it hides and escapes

and stays still
under its hood of rock

amid a galore of graves
and green leaves,

spring of fresh water
beside the sea,

a find, a treasure,
a pedigree,

no idyll
but the essential source,

now retired
from its work of sole sustenance,

living among memories
of former fame,

a saint's hand dipping in
like a taper unquenched,

coins splashing down
for reverence, not luck,

from time to time,
a self baptism,

secret and quick,
for some

prefer their ritual
out of doors,

water understands this,
and loves the brow

fanned with its body
for reasons the water easily guesses,

for it is the one who blesses,
freely,

freely it runs
its long unceremonious

caress
through my fingers,

and on my lips
tastes ferriferous,

blood-hint at the periphery,
pell-mell mint at the heart.

Waiting

Here are some clouds
waiting for their painter,
who is not yet born.

And fragrant leafy little parks,
rivers also who wait for their painter.

So many things are waiting,
so many summers.

Their painter is but far-off cascades
and undergrowths,

Lac Virginis,

not yet grown into pains,
still far-fetched,
innocent as a window,

or the consent of mountains.

Overhead,
a cloud no one can afford to buy,
priceless relic, unpainted.

Door

A door takes care not to,
no one can make it,
as the open page promised –
but what appeared, appeared,
like the Middle Ages
in a history lesson, all its birds
and shadows. A door,
like a usual ocean, and the long
pardonable movement of it in the world,
at this very moment,
left alone to be itself, after all,
where it belongs,
as stretching to it afterwards
will not work,
nor the entangled steps
have a kind word to say,
for it is a leaf's
experience of a tree,
trying to belong,
as all do.

Ideal Goat

Ram of rams,
prosperous beast,

golden fleece,
furnace beast,

commissioner of mysteries,
scape beast,

when young a lamb
and sacrificed,

when old a ram
and mighty,

beast conceived
by a lily,

coolly-nipped
between her burning thighs.

A Leaf Out of His Book

1
Cool climate;
a light frost followed
by the removal by thieves
of several large valuable clouds.

2
A day of rain and peacocks,
warm glooms,
some vanishings
and some tetherings.

3
Pearly manes
leaving behind
only their shadows
at dusk.

4
The first age of rain.
Taller and taller
its ladders
holding up the sky.

5
On some days
a single voyage
translates as:
tears.

6

A leaf out of his book.
So the happier it made me.
A cloud of unrewarded rain.
My young utopian,
our child in China, so far away.
Twenty years ago to this day
her life sprang in me, new.
Her sweet mirth began.

7

Vapours, odours, woodlands.
Cool lovely times.
Original unity.
Slender downy branches
spreading upward.
Woodlands, odours, vapours.
Wet jasmine pastures,
the ashy rose.
Evening, netted and green-tailed.
And the light
holding its breath.
Bright fragments of world
still shining among the dust.
Powers exhaustible
and inexhaustible.

Songs of Prince O

1

Up in the mountains
Prince O
on a rain-buying expedition.

Make rain fall on my fields,
Rain-Merchant,

let the fields
of my neighbour prince
be dust,

speak to the clouds.

(A dollar a shower
O Prince O
before I speak to the clouds).

2

Sleeping as a woman,
waking as a man,

aged General Ho
with his six alacritous horses

rides proudly past
the Palace of Abstinence.

3

The moon carries sleep
all round the world,

luminous concubines
guide the morning rain

towards Prince O,

clouds conjugal,
clouds sororal.

In the gardens of Prince O
the friends of the poor

are already awake
in their spiced and brilliant

rainy thousands.

4

. . . who
from his best cloud
pours out
rain

bright
as the silky blue upper-class
pantaloons

of an Imperial tutor?

5

No more
(sings Prince O)
mauvais airs,
no more sucettes

or bains sentis.

But Prince O
also sings:

M'pralé kéyi fèy mwê,
I am going to pick my leaves,

feuilles, feuilles . . .

leaves,
come save me
from shadow brides
and watercolour wives,

from all ghosts,
feuilles, feuilles . . .

6

Prince O breathes
through his lunar nostril
like young Buddha
practising archery.

He writes on peony petals
with a borrowed brush.

He hides no meanings.

Mud

Somewhere they are still drowning newborn daughters,
somewhere in teashops

there are posters which read:
PLEASE DO NOT DISCUSS POLITICS. DO NOT DO IT.

Somewhere, someone remains beautiful
as she somersaults into sleep,

into dreams of dextrous dissent,
of basic masquerade,

where a revolutionary army rises from the mud,
leaping like frogs.

Geologies

Oily lustre of peridot
                 river gravels
                      and beach sands
Bluish moonstones
               amber boulders
                      small natural pearls
Layers around tiny cores
                 stairs of ammonite
                         (crystal faces
like crystal ghosts
            that appear
                  as another mineral
settles on the crystal faces
                during a pause
                     in its growth)
Warm mineral–rich water
                circulating in open spaces
                           underground
A mass of fossil nautiloids
               soft black graphite
                        hard white diamond
Long clear angular crystals
             of quartz
                  within larger pink
feldspar grains
          Aventurine feldspar
                 or sunspot
with spangled reflections
             produced
                by the metallic crystals inside
Silky sheen of tiger's eye
             Ruin marble
                 with its pattern
of light and dark components
             that
                give it the sepia and parchment

appearance
    of a ruined city scape
                    or the old churches of Moscow
Bright rich green of malachite
            crushed to powder
                        as cosmetic pigments
in the Bronze Age of Egypt:
            Aragonite
                Flowers of iron
Fossilized sea lilies
        Rhodonite –
            implicitly Greek for rose
Massive blue sodalite
        intense blue of Sapphiris
                    unfading jade,
pale lucky jade
        Lapis lazuli
            for making bowls
or Chinese belt-hooks
            and
            coming from sulphur molecules in the rock,
used by Pharaohs
        and the Kings of Ur
                but not simulants
or imitations,
        stained jasper
            recognized by its Prussian
not ultramarine tint:
        jasper
            iaspis
                iashm
                yashp
                    ashpu
Waterworn crystals of smoky quartz
                citrines
                    and honey citrines
Precious opal
        with its play of iridescence
                (Common opal

or upala

        has none)

                Pale reddishness of a fire opal

Water opal

           clear and colourless as tears

                        veins of blue opal

nodules of fire opal

             vein of pale orange

                     and whitish opal

in the matrix of the rock

                interpenetrant crystals

                       of purple fluorite

Quartz rosettes

          skyblue turquoise

                  pierre turquoise

or Turkey stone

          for it came on those trade routes

                       Viennese turquoise

is fake

       and so is 'Neolith'

               or German turquoise

Angular blue grains

         in a pale matrix

                 Rubies of Burma

Cornflower blue

         of the sapphires

            of Kashmir

Peridot greens

        like the leaves of waterlilies

                  Olivine also,

its bright green waterworn fragments:

               Serpentinization

                     of the rocks

into shamrock,

        leaves cut into serpentine

               misleadingly called

Styrian Jade:

       iridescent cabochons,

             pebbles

of jasper or iaspis
                    Ghosts within,
                                    as when
the growth of a quartz crystal
                            is interrupted,
                                          resulting
in the formation
                  of a 'phantom crystal'
                                within a larger host,
like a mountain
                looming
                        inside a mountain . . .

                        *

A hollow box of siderite
                  that then becomes
                              lined
with crystals
            of at–first clear
                      then milky quartz
a jagged or hackly edge sometimes
                        of thin sheets
                              or shaped
like tiny steps
            Satin spar
                  a variety of gypsum
quite soft
            greenish radiating needles on slate
                            a fine tarnish
on the crystal
            of a crust of dark blue crystals
                            'piedras de rayo'
seagreen swirling smaragdite
                      Alabastra
                        for the ointment vases
of Egypt
            Saccharoidal marbles
                    of the Taj Mahal

chalcedony
          agate
                    onyx
                         chrysoprase
                                   carnelian
Amethysts
          from the gem gravels
                              of Sri Lanka
the shine of Bluejohn
                    like cloud scrolls unfurling
                                             Snowball white
of polished
          orbicular rock
                         Nodules of flint
Heartred rubies
               Iron-bright blue of sapphires
                                             Green
transparent waterfall sparkle
                              of aquamarine
                                             as if light
lived only here
               within the pure
                              and flawless stone
Fans of hornblende crystals
                         Silvery prisms of mispickel
                                                  with
a little quartz
               and very pale green cubes of fluorite
                                             as well as
tiny dirty-looking globules
                         of chlorite
                                   on a veinstone
containing copper pyrite
                    and fluorite
                              Also grey copper ore
composed of innumerable
                    thin plates
                              shot

in various directions
                of the pigeon-neck colour
                                in the outer
thin coat
        capillary crystals of Kirwan
                        of a light brown colour
like the finest hair
           or spun glass
                    of such a tender form
it is almost impossible
               to move it in its natural state
without injury
           Feathered gypsum
                  or snow fossil
Sky-blue copper ore
           lengthened into parallelograms
                            a little
transparent
        and perfect in the forms
                  intermixed
with copper
        of a grassgreen colour
                    Creamy white cacholong
on quartz
        an opaque form of opal
                  easily identified
as it adheres
        to the tongue
                A thin dark crust
of chalcedony
        'greedy of water'
                  Wafer-thin hexagonal plates
of calcite
        with a little bronze chalybite
                      on quartz
Copper of satin white
        in undulated form
                  in a rich stone

of various colours

                 Dark blue radiating masses

                                 of clinoclase

in an iron-rich veinstone

                      Copper of the lightest green

                                     instellated

forms and globular fragments

                   Velvet-green olivine

                               phosphate

of iron and copper

                in fine sheaf-like groups

                         of dark-green minute prisms

Skeleton chalcedony

               like 'an agglutinated mass

                         of cylindrical

bones of small birds'

               Black crystals of tin ore

                     (as if set)

indistinct crystals

           in a plate of dark-coloured

                      mica

Thin blade-like crystals

             of selenite

                textbook crystals

of white orthoclase feldspar

              with pale smoky

                  quartz

Applegreen copper

         tufts of golden

              olivinite

laths

   of grey wolframite

           on white quartz

lumps of arsenic

      in a vein

         up to eight feet wide

traversing the greenstone

          Grey shining entangled

               needles of quartz

crystals of quartz
                surrounded
                       by silvery prisms
of arsenopyrites
                nests of crystals
                       a forest
of milky quartz crystals
                    minute quartz crystals
                              giving
a sugary effect
            Brickred jasper
                  on kaolinized granite
From the mine dumps in autumn
                        quartz
                          with a small hollow
containing
           minute brown
                 nadorite
and
    colourless blades
              of valentinite
Mica roses
          on rock crystal –
                  their stiff delicate
aggregated star-bursts
              in clefts and cavities
                     both
anticipating
          and remembering
                the rose –
perhaps
       not
        accidentally . . .

This poem is indebted to the Geology Museum, South Kensington, London, and to the Royal Cornwall Museum, Truro.

A Guide to Masks and Fans

MASKS

The real people
            of the Arctic
                        have much leisure time
in their long winters
                to prepare sun and moon masks
                                        for any shaman:
Mask of the Moon Spirit
                    made of
                            ptarmigan's claw,
raven's beak
            and feathers of good fortune,
                                    or the animal soul mask
owl or whale
            enclosing
                    a human mask within:
The chorusing women
                of the Arctic
                            raise their hands
garnished with fingermasks
                    In Gurunsi
                            they like
broad butterfly masks
                In the rain forest
                            masks
are for mourning
                each takes six months to prepare,
is conical,
            reaches down
                    to the wearer's chest
and has no eyeholes,
                for the fabric of the masks –
                                        barkcloth –
has been beaten
            to see-through
                    translucence:

But they bear facial features,
                    are painted
                              in a geometry
of black and brown,
                    dead kinsfolk
                              visiting the living
via these bereavement masks:
                    Here is a mask
                              of the water spirit
disguised as an antelope
                    horns
                              fountaining up
and the owner of the mask
                    may carve
                              a miniature version
of his mask
          to take on journeys
                    as emissary of the main mask,
though nowadays
                    many masks
                              are made with an eye to the art market

                              *

Cow
    bird
        monkey
            leopard
                caribou
                    fish
                        pig and owl:
all appear on masks
                    throughout the world
                              Some people
only wear masks
          for weddings
                    others only for funerals,

others
            merely to dance-demonstrate
                        the slight,
the imperceptible difference
                        between
                        good and evil:
But to the English
            mask means horse
                        with hinged jaws for clattering
as in 1948
            when Harvey May tease-danced
                        before the Peace 'Oss,
his beak-mask
            a co-ordination
                        of red, black and white angles
to reflect
            the bigger snapping Oss-face –
                        coalshine, fireblaze,
prodigal white of snow and ice –
                        true dragon stare
                                    The crouch-dancer
with ribboned wand
            up-held
                        in a brandish of place, staring back:
All masks are best seen
            when danced
                        whether at Padstow
or at Guinea-Bissau
            where small children
                        wear fish
or dog masks
            and the adolescents
                        graduate to bull and shark
Here
            only the children wear masks
                        Being grown-up here
means
            not wearing a mask
                        a false face

*

Here is Cardinal Wolsey
                pictured holding an orange
                              and wearing
a Cardinal Wolsey mask
                Whereas in a non-tudor
                        culture
men of high rank
            prefer
                masks covered with spiders' web
or the little candid
              skull-crowned masks
                      of Buddhist deities
or the ghost masks
              of the Noh stage
                  competing in magnificence
with the brocade robes
              of the actors
                  especially
the 'young woman' mask
              delicate enough
                  to register
any true emotion
            Whereas
                in the palace of the Ogoga of Ikere-Ekitu
they don full-height
              administrator masks
                to mock the British

*

'In his hand
           he holds an object
                that strikes the spectator
at first
    simply
          as some obscure, some ambiguous work of art,

111

but that
          on second view
                    becomes a representation
of a human face,
          modelled and coloured,
                         in wax,
in enamelled metal,
          in some substance
                    not human.'

                    *

The most potent mask
          comes from wood
                    taken without killing the tree
'The mask was painted red
          if work
                    on the carving
began in the morning
          and black
                    if carving began in the afternoon'
They repaint
          the masks
          each spring
Even the symptoms-of-illness masks
                    the masks
                         as passports
the miniature masks
          made to serve as witnesses
                    to important events
Women in hood masks
          with beadwork faces
                    sway their heads
from side to side
          moving slowly
                    into the past
Or there are masks
          with shell eyes
                    and serene faces

to portray the female dead
                                You want a fiercer look?
                                                        Try
this grinning mask
                of a sorcerer
                                officiating at a funeral in Bali,
or this mask
                of a money-lender
                                or this mask
which lay in a cave
                for over two thousand years
                                                half human,
half jaguar
                made of plain wood
                                with snarling jade around the mouth
or the grim perfume masks
                of plague doctors,
                                        or masks only
to be worn
                during an eclipse
                                (or veils, those ghosts of masks)

                                *

So many masks carved
                from what the dreamer saw
                                                sleeping,
one mask so richly jewelled
                        the wearer
                                'might have been
king of the world':
                But whether the mask
                                is made of gold
or paper
                cowhide or silver
                                snakeskin or silk
above all
                it is the mask's sense of eloquence
                                        we admire:

113

FANS

Hot weather invents the fan
                             Flies, pesky buzzers,
                                         insects
all very swattable
                  invent
                       require the fan
Indeed
         the oldest surviving fan
                         in the Western World
is Queen Theodolinda's Fan,
                     a flabellum,
                          actually –
to keep flies
               off the Host:
                     But Elizabeth the First
had twenty-seven fans
                     'one fanne of white feathers
                              with a handle
of golde
            having two snakes
                     wyndinge about it,
embellished
              with a ball of diamonds
                        in the end . . .'
But the eighteenth century
                  is the era
                     of the fan
A world
         assembles
               to be painted upon them:
Birds and roses
            Views of Bath
                  Pompeian frescoes of Youth and Age,
piqued with gold
              Fan painted
                  with an allegory of the marriage

of Louis XIV –
                cupids are making the bed –
                                A simple scene
of shepherd
            and shepherdess
                        The head of Goliath
amid a scene
            of sequined fountains:
                                fans of silk,
of satin,
        of 'chickenskin'
                        (by which is meant
unborn babyskins
                from aborted children)
                                The guardsticks
set
    with articulated vignettes
                        of two men sawing a plank
and a girl
            picking flowers:
                        a *trompe l'oeil* fan
painted
        with an invitation
                    to the Ball
at the Mansion House,
                a lottery card,
                            and a bank draft
for ten pounds:
            A man holding a birdcage:
                                A lady
with an exaggerated
                eighteenth-century
                            coiffure
in whose height
            a fortified castle
                    with cannon, war tents
and regimental banners
                is courageously
                        giving battle:

An engraving of Apollo
                         resting his horses,
                                        fans
rich in allegory,
                  elaborate Spanish fans,
                                     one showing
the triumphal entry
                   of Don Carlos Bourbon
                                       into Naples:
Ladies watching over babies
                         lying in a nest
                                    of eggshells,
the verso with gardeners resting,
                              seven views
                                      of Margate,
a misty scene of nymphs
                      by a lily pond,
                                  this painted fan
on which a lady
             lifts a mask
                       to her face:
Horoscope fans
             for telling fortunes,
                                 fans giving instructions
for dancing
           the latest dances
                           or for playing whist:
Waterfall fans
              A taffeta fan
                         in the form of a cockade
opening to 360 degrees,
                     with guards
                               to form handles,
the sticks tortoiseshell,
                     the leaf
                           fashioned
of bands of green,
                 yellow
                     and brown silk

with silver lace –
                    this is the fan
                                   of Mary, Queen of Scots:
A handful of scrap fans
                         augmented
                                   with extra ostrich down,
articulated fans,
                  the movement
                                pushes a parrot out
to peek-peck at a lady:
                       a Brazilian fan
                                       or handscreen
of rainbow feathers
                    decorated
                             with stuffed hummingbirds –
green feathers
              from the Quetzal,
                                purple feathers
from the Cotingas,
                   sold at auction in 1986
                                            for £2600:
Fans
     depicting plans
                      of forthcoming military manoeuvres,
'Fans unfolding history',
                          picturing
                                    the Birth of the Dauphin,
then later,
           the costumes of the Revolution,
                                            fifteen figures
dressed
        in the official robes
                               of the revolutionary government,
crudely-coloured,
                  as is
                       the educational fan titled
Grammaire Française
                     à l'usage
                               des Rentiers:

117

Fans celebrating
                    ballooning exploits
                                        or memorializing
The 1800 Act of Union
                    of England,
                                        Scotland and Ireland:
'Fair Sister Isles . . .
                    blest
                        as free . . .'
Not forgetting church fans
                            with suitable subject –
though one parishioner
                        shocks
                                by absentmindedly
or maliciously
            unfurling
                        her fan of naked cupids:

                            *

Fans are mostly made
                    by women
                                and therefore anonymous:
but there is also
                the useful anonymity
                                    of fan shelter,
providing
        fan partners
                    with welcome seclusion

                            *

A last burst of fans
                    early this century –
                                    mostly
for advertising purposes,
                        e.g., Agence Cook –
                                        with a view

of the Grand Hotel
de la Gare
du quai d'Orsay,
or for perfumes
in which case
the fans were scented:
And nowadays?
an epidemic of fans:
Four fan sales a year
at Christie's . . .
My favourite?
This fan printed
with
'A new Game of Piquet Now in Play
Among Different Nations
in Europe:
ten women representing
France
Spain
Sardinia
Austria
Saxony
Portugal
Russia
Poland
Brittania
and Holland
seated round a table
with all
except the last three
taking hands
in a game of piquet,
Pope Innocent XI
present
but declining to take part
although his chair is at the ready':
the fan symbolizes
'The intrigues
of nineteenth-century diplomacy

119

concerning
        the affairs of Poland':
                a bold polemic of fanhood,
though not perhaps
        a fan
           to take with you to the Opera.

For information, quotations and adapted quotations in the above I am indebted to the following:

Timothy Teuten, *The Collector's Guide to Masks* (Bracken Books, 1995)

Susan Mayor, *The Letts Guide to Collecting Fans* (Charles Letts, 1991)

Joseph Campbell, *The Masks of God* (Secker and Warburg, 1965)

The quoted passage beginning 'In his hand he holds an object' is from *The Sacred Fount* by Henry James

Holidays

Like a Neptunist
on holiday in a desert resort,
gambling and partying,
taking a break from water,
or a Plutonist
who, escaping her own incandescence,
retreats to the Arctic,
or a metal
that hovers for centuries
between iron and silica,

overnight the daylight
breaks away,
escaping with all its
latitudes and longitudes
and its rivers
still fast asleep in its arms
to where it will re-write history
using the sudden and unexpected
coherence of haiku,
a form of poetry

which must always
be written out of doors,
'Shasei',
and as that day gets going,
full of hope,
it passes my school-leaver Dad
out on his bike
delivering drought warning leaflets
all around the quiet sunstruck
streets of pre-war Egham and Staines.

Comet H.B.

No reckless rider,
no Filippi dei Adimari
on one of his stampeding war horses,

silver sparks shooting from iron shoes:
no, seeing the comet
at the end of our lane

is to see a friend of long-standing
or long-flying,
returning after much journeying

around so many watching worlds,
angel with mane of ice and gas,
star-kite hovering, wondrous

good-luck visitor,
illuminant not gargoyle,
gyroscopic talisman,

visionary bearer
from world to world
of the hot seeds of life,

scattering them equally
on the fertile and the barren lands,
gratis,

'a deliberate dispersive act':
out of the windfall night
the husbandry of a heavenly body.

News Item, 30 January 1998

On the day a Frenchman
takes six salamanders into space
I find on the front page

a picture, green and sorrowful,
of a recently-restored gargoyle
at Salisbury Cathedral.

The Frenchman has gourmet rations,
kilos of quail in grape sauce –
up in space

he'll feed like a dandy in Proust,
while just a year and a bit's spit
away from Mir

the solar eclipse moons in the wings,
solar gargoyle thinking of us,
having at its core great plans,

burning to get first to England,
darken it good, then on to France.
And those fiery French amphibs?

Six coals taken further
but just as surplusly as to Newcastle.

Spilsbury's Invention

Spilsbury's jigsaws
began as 'dissected maps',
the cheaper ones 'without the sea'.

It became a social skill.
'Just think, Mama,
she is unable to put the map of Europe together.'

First, puzzle-maps;
twenty years later, portraits of English monarchs,
for the 'instruction of youth'.

Rational amusement for all ages
in the halcyon days of the jigsaw.

Soon you could choose
between *Pilgrim's Progress*
or a more contemporary event:

Edward Oxford, in 1840, say,
firing at her Majesty
as she rode in her carriage through the Park.

Sources: the essay 'Joys of the Jigsaw' by Linda Hannas, in *The Saturday Book*, No 29.
'Just think, Mama . . .': Jane Austen, *Mansfield Park*.

Angels

For angels pray just like other creatures
as they 'walk upon the wings of the world'
or carry vases of water about
without any look of indignation,
or wait, patient and detached,
as the artist,
no longer interested in realist details,
goes rapidly from century to century,
painting what amounts
to the unification of souls
in a landscape of affinity, where all memories
are one memory,
all trees the one same tree shaken with light,
and every path
is the one that always pleaded
to be noticed,
for it is the beginning of the landscape
across which angels are preparing to travel
towards whoever will come to meet them,
entranced experts or tranquil deserters,
along such earliest simplest trajectories as theirs.

The Rose

All the white roses in Eden
blushed red at Eve's beauty,

and in The Empress's library-garden
over two hundred roses
bushelled over trellises, arcades, arbours . . .

Chinese rosetrees
carried to Europe on the tea clippers,

for 'such was the international regard
for the rose'
that victorious English captains

sent on to the enemy
the roses destined for Josephine –

no olive branch,
but for the sake of the rose,
as Cleopatra drenched her sails with rose-water,

her fragrant barge travelling amusk –
and as here among the meek graves
at backwater Budoc

a late yellow rose – distant cousin
to Mrs Oakley Fisher – its roots among bone,
sends up to us

tireless edgeways puffs of perfume,
shirrs and chiffons of scent,
utterance of rose, as in Eden.

The quotation above is from *Scents and Sensuality: The Essence of Excitement* (Max Lake, 1989).

Waterstone Whispers

Hi. Out of these swarms of books
why not let me be your own buzzing book,
your bible of the poor told in pictures,

or your humming sutras brought
so far, on foot, right,
from India to China, a twenty year walk?

No? Then surely you'd like me
to be your Liber Studiorum,
weather-stained pages of storm and shipwreck

for happy indoor voyages,
in fact, I'll be any kind of rough guide
to anywhere you like,

but I will not be a book of condolence,
like those Dianic books in which last autumn
so many wrote what they never dreamed they'd write.

But I will be your magic book from Mexico,
grimoire of painted thoughts
where the green-plumed raingod

lives inside his house of clouds,
his thunder-tower roofed with lightnings,
kind master to his favourite bird, the roseate spoonbill.

Don't go away bookless, spend that token,
let me be your paperback zen,
your wipeclean volume of occult cuisine,

even one of these lopsided anthologies,
if I must . . .

And you can be my papyrus,
my Tang Dynasty scroll, my Liber Amor,
for me alone to read with more than eyes,

big boy, lets be one instantly-open book,
lets get reading.

Ours

The path smelt sensible.
It made a bow, a dusty salaam.
It did not know it was coming back to me;

secretly it thirsted,
it came back,
it was in its wooden shoes.

The path came ploughing along,
I rested myself on it,
it was smiling and suffering.

Now and then we were one.
Or followed one another about,
in places where you hold your tongue.

If we were everybody or nobody
we didn't know. We were one.

Rainy Silences

Rainy silences
taking so much for granted

Evenings
under contract to the day after tomorrow

Indoor pearls
in the headquarters of the dark ages

As if a visitation almost came
speaking of itself

Like a reverie that had been in arrears
too long

Orchids

The secret of silver and gold
is darkness

but light is invented
to illuminate, for us,

the feet of the gods.
Look no higher.

Such cryptic
and provocative innocence

is enough; above
are plasms, milks and veils,

womb-light,
waxy-purples, greys

radiant beyond possibility.

Also
there are hours
in which you could grow orchids.

Indoors

House of invisible waterfalls,
indoor echoes,

the central heating
whistling through its teeth,

the born blind silences
of the window,

his themes of juniper
and fallen leaf,

a meanwhile of the self
coolly true and untrue,

a felicity of heartbreak,
the falls

chilling and scenting
the house

with brilliant musks
of the unseen,

the sanity
of their no-worse-for-wear floods.

Light

Of its own accord,
born, how is it
so strong and quick, like glass
suddenly a window,
a trace and a plunge,
a work like treason
but not treason, what is mistaken
curls up like a sandspout,
and it is better to be a velocity
like that when Friday
comes along like a wind
or a sad story quietly told,
triumphantly heard –
here are paths that live
greatly entire, and of their
own accord, move like
yourselves, succulent architects,
holding their tongues in the sun,
above all surprised by
the night coming of its own accord,
with much more to relate.

Sometimes the Spoken

Sometimes the spoken
is a paper pardon, hanging
in the trees like a thought
making its bow, just
as when it rains there is
quiet, there is something perfectly
done, but for how long,
a portrait hastened to see,
it might even have been pushed,
but what is seen is
walking away without a word,
a savant or a serpent
let out of a wish,
like a smile before a face is ready,
vagrant or sorrowful,
for too many selves are being born in it,
verdant with wants.

The Air Bell

I
The driest January for 200 years.
A veer of sun over icy Argal Water,
a snowfall of birds

on the greying water, settles as one bird,
replete;
laconic pink mist of buds on the far shore

of alders and crack willows –
Hopkins notes this same mist. To the west,
engineers are rebuilding the dam,

a steep white ziggurat waiting for cascades.
Argal's dimmed water has more light than the sky,
pours it up, propitious,

to help the sky;
on the cold slope, three horses twirl shyly about,
modelling their canvas shawls,

scatter birds lift off the water,
grey-white over white-grey . . . As we come down
close to the bouldered shore,

a high clear hidden bell rings out . . .
We search the stunt of evergreen bushes,
the muddle of myrtle,

even scratch about in the nearby half orchard . . .
Who's hung this bell on an unseen branch
to ring out with windshaken fidelity

over Argal's rocky water-shrine?
The wild bell chimes to us
like outstretched arms we cannot embrace . . .

We listen, no longer searching,
and the outdoor music follows us a little way
then is lost in the turn of the shore.

II
And months later I'm looking
at one of the oldest Pre-Reformation bells
in existence,

600 years old and enjoying retirement
in the side aisle of St Winwallow's sea-stained
and angel-porched church

where the last sermon in Cornish
was preached, to those with ears to hear . . .
a greenish barnacled upturned chalice of a bell,

cracked and silent,
though her younger cousins still sing out
up in the serpentine and granite tower.

Her old English script, with Lombardy Capitals, reads:
'Nomen Magdalene Gerit Compana Melodie'.
I spread an eavesdropping hand,

touch her seagreen cool metal,
this ancestress to the air bell of Argal,
and deep to my fingerbones I feel her song

tremoring through –
My name is Magdalene and I make melodious music.

St Nectan's Fall
(North Coast, Cornwall)

Slippery gentleman, St Nectan,
breathing his own weather,

raising his own lather,
custodian of spate,

of the long precipice drop
into his black begging bowl,

white water-rope, spurting cascade,
smolt and sluice of a reverse fountain

scouring round
the basalt belly of the kieve,

gimping, looping and zinging;
a water cauldron for a saint

or a luck bath for a travelling sagesse?

On the slippery ledge,
just a juniper branch to grip,

we peer in, down,
spray roaring on our faces,

maelstrom chant,
opera whirlpool in our ears,

for Nectan's whispering water-gallery
has secrets to squander-sing,

smooch-splashing and hiss-humming down
into the ever-spilling basin

of black and shagreen rock
from which a sunlit slab of water,

beck of bright gravels, runs,
little amatory river,

no Ganges, no Orinoco,
inch–deep, quickening down

greedy and humble through the wooded gorge,
a goblet gulping its secret way.

Dad's Dream, 1944

I was back at Wun Lun
and walking down the lane
to the Thai market stalls
but as I neared them
the scenery changed
and I was now going down
another lane
that led into the High Street
of my home town
and there, sitting on chairs
watching the passing traffic,
were all of my own
and my fiancée's families.
They greeted me
as though it were a perfectly normal
way to meet, and everybody
was intrigued
by the strange clothing I was wearing,
especially the huge blue patches
on my tattered khaki trousers.
My clompers, too, were of great interest
and there was much comment
about the moustache I had only started
to grow after capture.
Animated conversations were held
as I passed round some banana fritters
just purchased,
which were accepted without comment.
After a short while I made my apologies
and bade them goodbye,

Almost direct transcription of an account of his dream at Chungkai Camp given by my
father Jack Shuttle in his war memoir *Destination Kwai* which fully documents his experi-
ences as a Far-Eastern Prisoner of War.

Shortly after this dream, the prisoners received mail from home, the first letters and
parcels they'd received after almost two years of complete isolation.

Clompers are a sort of native clog, made from kapok.

pointing out that it was nearly six o'clock
and we were not allowed
by the Japs
to be in the market after this hour.

Houses: Nightingale, Fry, Brontë and Curie

I was in Curie,
though I'd've preferred Brontë –
the arts not the sciences my forte,

but I had much fondness for Fry;
as she toured the foul prisons
I felt the romance of it,

her goodness
like a clean starched apron
wrapping her,

I was there with her,
being kind to the degradant
and the savage,

sailing along at her side
down
dank dark corridors,

their stench much improved
by the wafts of dry protestant virtue
we brought . . .

I helped her bring her light to the dark . . .
And although
our netball team

beat hers time and again,
I still liked her the best.
Of all four,

Nightingale I thought least of,
her lovely name sang not to me,
I can't think why,

unless
it was that I had room in me
for only three heroines, max,

and she was just the unlucky loser.
But later,
long after school,

I liked to think of her
shipwrecked on her invalid sofa,
furiously thinking,

but doing nothing, nothing, nothing . . .
Its on the cards for any of us,
to just come home, like her,

from somewhere
terrible and extraordinary,
and give up –

though hardly an example to the girls.

One of Our Miniature Masterpieces

House inside a house,
seed of a house,
likeness-house sitting

on the palm of my hand,
with paradisal turrets
and many fingernail doors

inviting minuscule entry,
portals of possibility,
an ideal home,

if a trifle over-roofed,
extra-adumbrated
in those aspects of mimicry

suggesting a house Holmes
might have professionally
visited,

if he were tiny enough;
bosomed with bow windows,
responsibly-gabled,

circled by a garden of bowers
and steppingstone paths;
a small-scale mansion,

a minor palace of domestic peace,
micro-house where our macro hopes
of good days and better nights can shelter:

simplified quintessence of house,
homoeopathic abode,
with 'one of our miniature masterpieces'

scribed proudly by the manufacturer
on the green baize lawn concealed beneath.
This house you gave me

means in many different ways
somewhere difficult but delightful
to live;

easier to live in these prototypical rooms
than in our bigger frailer house
where

masterpiece making is not yet practised
upon such a scale
as in the gift house –

residence tiny yet vast with potential habitation.

Book, as Leopard

As in an old fable
a king of weather
lies hidden in a jewel

inventing
the very opposite of gold –
just to please you,

his regency
ebbing and flowing overhead
in the form of reclusive

but confident clouds,
so the book is stroking you
with quiet paws,

of its own accord:
it stands for me but
with much more magnificence,

like London seen far-off
from above,
through the struggle and luxury

of the clouds over Heathrow,
the river stepping out of
its own delicacy,

entering, if it likes,
my parents' house,
with certainty of welcome:

where lives young Leopard,
as book, as me,
turning our pages,

a whirlwind lying in state.

Selves

I shall see, shan't I, a river,
its torn glass going towards green,

at the very least, of its own accord,
going, or curled up like a trumpet trembling

in vain, such selves I do not wish,
or not yet, I do not wish to wheel round

in a whisper wholly above there,
holding sorrowfully and mistaken,

I shall see a tower by turns, shan't I,
feel its tinge

like so many of the wishing stations,
or smell, or taste all that it was suffering

in silent attempts to understand
a savant's thirst, of its own accord,

but like a sentence perpendicularly singing,
quiet among the open announcements

told in gusts,
as green replaced himself with questions:

that is why – driven, pushed,
the sentence appeared,

was lost sight of in the stormy least,
departed, went off everywhere,

spent the quiet day opening an umbrella,
a father lost to perfection,

who wept, said it was rain,
or perhaps a word spoken to everyone

from our selves
dumb among magnificent wolf books,

the torn glass emitting meanwhile
tongues to the hilt, sea-green tongues after all,

as if glad, very glad, to speak
unburdening dialects back

into the river's sated gleam –
such selves I have not wished.

Also

1
Thumb of light
hitching a weekday cloud.
Turning into something sweeter.

But, the muse of tears
also.

2
Also,
the azure, sighing.
Daybreak waters.

3
Those sanctuaries are ours.
The oversoul's dark
health.
Also, fortresses of cloud,
weather-stained.

4
Also, quiet ambushes.
The moon resting her horns
on her breast.

White blossom bursts
from the pebbled root.

5

Cloud-gatherers, whose success
is assured. Rain

already a mist above the waters.

Also,
wet bright air, day
afloat and shining, Horoskopos.

6

Also, a plant
whose leaves curve downward,
whose leaflets
fold together at nightfall
or when touched.

7

The glory of spirality –
water's solitary joys.

And
a grasshopper
hitching a ride on a chameleon's back.

8

Harvested hills
of red and gold,

evening brambles,
bright glooms
before the darkness.

9

Stars also, brightly-
torn from the verbatim sides of the world.

Comock's Journey

When everything they had
fell through the sea-ice floor,
they ate their dogs.

Their best dogs they saved,
and fed them on the dog leftovers.

'The voice said, Cry.'

They ate their dogs
because sea ice ate their rations,
their lamps, harpoons and spears,
their snow knives.

'What shall I cry?'

Out of nothing but snow and tradition
Comock and his family
rebuilt home and arctic hearth,

bred up more dogs.
It took years . . . nightless days,
dayless nights . . . At last

they travelled on (what choice?)
in a driftwood, dogbone and sealskin umiak,
sailing back

towards the Ungava Peninsula,
giving famous Flaherty one helluva
surprise . . .

'Forgive our rags, our shitty little boat . . .'
The entire family, laughing –
'private joke, Bob, between us and the ice.'

The story of the survival of Comock and his family is re-told in *Arctic Dreams* by
Barry Lopez (Picador, 1986).

Under the Weather
for P

Weighing a cloud in your hand,
just like a common person

or the worst traveller ever,
brushing aside the pine forest,

dreading a planetary shower,
a rainy appreciation.

Weighing a swamp, or France,
or the nick of time,

or an old woe. I love you.

Utamaro

At the dimlit Utamaro exhibition
an old wheelchair man

nods over the smeared-glass cases –
spotting the first batch

of erotica
creak-leaps to his feet

(ignoring the protests
of his companion)

drinking-in
the vigour and grief-reducing

splendour of Utamaro's lovers,
scoop and grab of flesh

seen, smelt too,
through convulsive drifts and crumples

of garment –
regional orange fading

to black honey,
clitoridal pinks darkly streaming,

wet-orchard green –
such fabrics, brocades, spilling

satins, outbursts
of motif, elegances

pushed aside, flung back
aslither

to display the embowered
prick

lodged in the geisha's sex
or jewel-casket,

her face alight,
sly, drowsy, thankful, serious –

for the lotus grows in mud!

Greedily the old invalid gazes
till his frowning girl

(daughter, wife, grandchild, nurse?)
whispers him away,

he and his reminiscent grunts
are wheeled away fast

from the gallery,
from this portal of pleasure . . .

Riddle

Many creatures don't have one.
But I have two.
Each one is a loner, but lives with four brothers.
How well in a cradle this creature soothes.

Our Backwater

Leaf-glitter
on railway bushes,

sun–glint
on wild celery,

emerald lichen
and manifest bracken,

without demands,
a caress from the truly naked –

careless glades of green,
sweet shambling round-trip train –

o advantages of circumnavigation,
april-fragrant thunders,

shifts of succulent light,
green-leaf triumph

even now
still pouring through

chinks
in the celestial arrangement . . .

After Red

I take off my red robe,
my carnival coat,
rich and beautiful apparel
whose caress and courage served me well.

I fold them away without regret.
I loved their cocksure ways
but now I want something less ornate,
to dress in colours that say —

'we are the dusks and silvers,
we are what comes after red,
your ruby reds,
your cache of bloodred fashions;

we are not wild or ardent,
lack red's festive instinct,
we are eclipses and jets,
bring no blessing;

our sole gift —
the benefit of the doubt.'

Dew

'Awake and sing,
ye that dwell in dust;
for thy dew
is as the dew of herbs,
and the earth
shall cast out her dead',
says Isaiah:
so on their way
Virgil washes
the face of the poet
with the dew that in another story
restores sight
to the blind girl Truth.